What Lies at the Heart of Genesis

What Lies at the Heart of Genesis

Mark Eddy Smith

lovesanarchy.com
TAMWORTH, NH

For my father,
who accepted responsibility.

Third Edition

©2020 by Mark Eddy Smith

www.lovesanarchy.com

This work is licensed under the Creative Commons Attribution-Noncommercial-No Derivative Works 3.0 United States License. To view a copy of this license, visit http://creativecommons.org/licenses/by-nc-nd/3.0/us/ or send a letter to Creative Commons, 171 Second Street, Suite 300, San Francisco, California, 94105, USA.

Anarchy symbol & crucifix: istockphoto.com
Ram silhouette: Adobe Stock

ISBN: 978-1-939636-50-8

Scripture quotations, unless otherwise noted, are from the New Revised Standard Version of the Bible, copyright 1989 by the Division of Christian Education of the National Council of the Churches of Christ in the USA. All rights reserved.

Contents

Timeline 8
Propositional Assumptions about God 11
Propositional Assumptions about Genesis 12
Chapter One: The Summer 13
Chapter Two: The Fall 25
Chapter Three: The Winter 39
Chapter Four: The Spring 53

Timeline

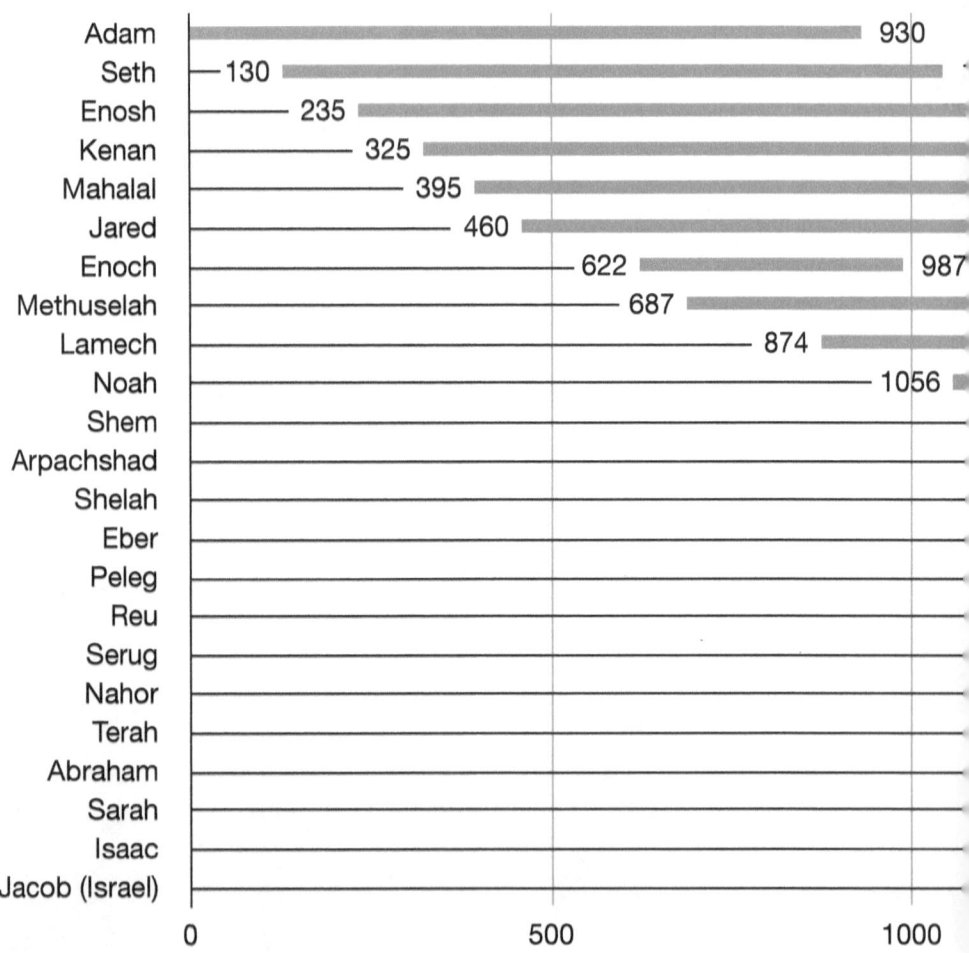

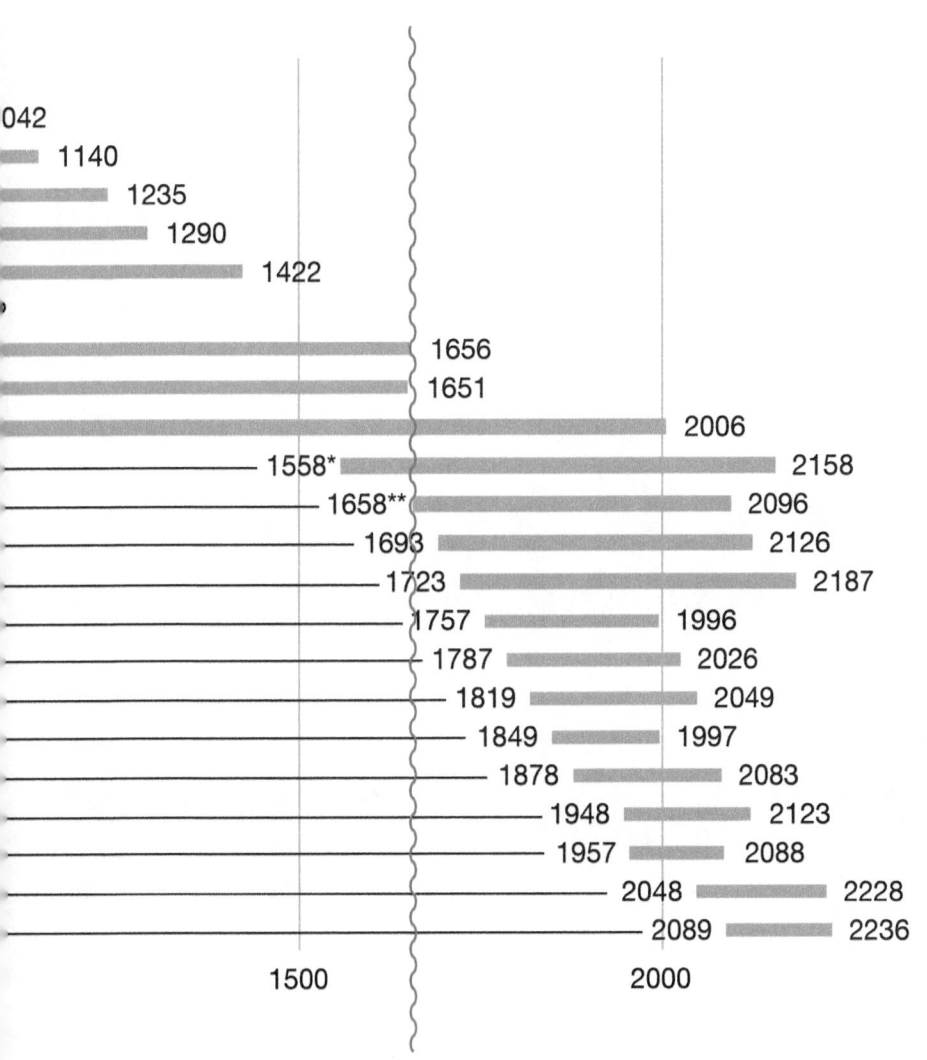

*"After Noah was 500 years old, Noah fathered Shem, Ham, and Japheth" (Gen. 5:32).

**"When Shem was 100 years old, he fathered Arpachsad two years after the flood" (Gen. 11:10).

Propositional Assumptions *about* God

1. You are you.

2. You identify with everyone.

3. You accept responsibility for everything.

4. You are incarnate in anyone who identifies with you.

5. You glory in vulnerability.

Propositional Assumptions *about* Genesis

1. It reveals your heart.

2. It tells damnable lies.

3. You accept responsibility for it all.

Chapter One:
The Summer

The myth of a six-day creation is only a lie if you take it literally. But what if it literally took six days to tell?

A SHEPHERD IS ON HIS BACK IN the middle of the night, gazing at the stars and wondering from whence it all came. The stars, the grass, the sheep—himself in the midst of them—how and why did it all come to be? His grandson has been asking such questions, but how can the shepherd possibly answer? Did some god make it all out of navel lint? Are the stars themselves gods? Or are they simply pinpricks in the sky through which some greater glory from beyond the heavens dimly sparkles?

For some reason the question has been building in urgency, and this night he cries out as loud as he can, "Is anyone there?" The silence that follows seems stern, punctuated only by the restive gruntings of his sheep, but then a voice, just on the edge of hearing and seeming to come from everywhere at once, says, "I am." The old man had heard stories of a god who walked with his ancestors, but he had never truly believed them.

"Who are you?" he asks, almost too softly to hear. Again the voice responds, "I am." The sound is so exactly the same as before that the shepherd suspects it's just some trick of the wind (in the shepherd's language it sounds like "Yaaah-waaay").

Conscious that he's asking in a way that will illicit the answer he desires, he nevertheless says, "Are you the one who created everything?"

"I am."

The shepherd has one more question and little hope that it will be answered. "How?"

The wind subsides, and the shepherd mutters, "I'm getting old." He snuggles deeper into his cloak and tries to sleep.

You, meanwhile, are pondering how best to answer his question. The man has no knowledge of either astro- or quantum physics. He doesn't have a word to describe a length of time longer than a few generations of his family. Evolutionary biology? The man barely understands how his sheep were domesticated. The periodic table of elements would mean as much to him as a review of *The Matrix*. All the man knows is what he can see and hear, and yet, you have been longing for someone with whom to converse, and there he lies, vulnerable and unafraid. You decide to take another risk. Just before he falls asleep, you translate his spirit to a time long ago and say, in a voice as soft as you can muster:

"In the beginning, when I was creating the heavens and the earth . . ."

As if in a dream, the shepherd is standing nowhere. All is utterly dark, but a salty, acrid wind tousles his hair and whistles in his ears. Your voice continues, a calm and reassuring presence: ". . . the earth was a formless void and darkness covered the face of the deep, while my spirit swept over the face of the waters."

And so, for awhile, there is nothing but wind and presence, until it seems as though the world has always been this way, and always will. As the silence deepens, the sense of a comforting presence fades, leaving the shepherd feeling at first alone, then forlorn, then possibly not alone but surrounded by less-comforting presences. The impenetrable darkness, the chaotic whistle and howl of the winds that assault him from every direction fills him with dread, until at last he is crouching with his hands over his head, wracked with rasping sobs. Within this interminable torment, your voice speaks again:

"Let there be light."

It's faint, at first, but it slowly grows in intensity, from gray to pale yellow to blinding white, so that his eyes begin to hurt. But there's nothing to see: He's standing in sun-drenched mist.

"Night," says the voice, "and day."

Again, the silence stretches, and again he feels alone, but this time his fear is different. Although he can't see anything, no evil could possibly hide in this impenetrable light. He is filled instead with a powerful sense of awe.

"See how good that is," says the voice.

When the shepherd awakes, the eastern horizon is paling, and his sheep are beginning to stir. He is as exhausted as if he'd kept watch all night with a pregnant ewe, but elated also, as though another lamb had been birthed into the world.

He spends the day in an unusually pensive mood. The sheep have plenty of grass, the predators in the area have enough food to allow them the luxury of avoiding shepherds. What else is he going to do but think on the dreams of the night? If dream it was. If vision, it was simple enough. Nothing revelatory. Except for the existence of the voice, of course. Still, it may have been nothing but a dream.

Night and day: they exist because the voice called them into being. It's more than he knew the day before.

In the evening, the shepherd returns his sheep to the same cranny in the hillside where they had rested the night before, hoping for another visitation.

He does not have long to wait. As soon as the western horizon grows dark, he finds himself back in the brilliant mist, and the voice is speaking.

"Let there be a dome in the midst of the waters, and let it separate the waters from the waters."

Immediately, the mist begins to lift. It becomes cloud cover, and the shepherd finds himself standing unsupported upon rolling waves.

"Sky," says the voice.

For the rest of the night (though it is day in the vision), the shepherd gazes at clouds and water, his spirit quickening with the hope that more may be revealed, but your voice signals the end of the vision by saying, "See how good it is to view the horizon," and he finds himself once more on the hillside with dawn approaching.

He spends this day composing the story he will tell his grandson about what he's being shown. He's beginning to believe the visions will continue, and the phrase that comes to mind is, "And there was evening, and there was morning, the second day." He imagines the eyes of his grandson sparkling as the secrets of the world's genesis are finally revealed.

The day is long, but at last the sheep are gathered together on the side of the hill, grazing contentedly. The shepherd leans against a tree and waits for the sun to set.

To his delight, he finds himself once more astride endlessly rolling waves. The voice wastes no time in speaking.

"Let the waters under the sky be gathered together into one place, and let the dry land appear."

The swell that rises beneath the shepherd is more massive than any previous wave, and when it subsides he is standing on bare rock.

"Earth," says the voice.

The water recedes some distance, then starts to return, only to crash upon the rock and recede.

"Seas," says the voice.

He assumes there will be nothing more created this third day, and resigns himself to another long night's watch, but the voice speaks on.

"Let the earth put forth vegetation: plants yielding seed, and fruit trees of every kind on earth that bear fruit with the seed in it."

The shepherd has never seen a time-lapse movie, so he doesn't quite grasp the fact that he's seeing the world at hyperspeed, green and gray erupting over bare rock, advancing and retreating like the waves, eating away at stone until grasses and ferns appear, whipping about as if in a gale, growing and dying almost too quickly to see. Slowly the flora rises until it blocks his view of the sea. Trees tower over him, hung with moss and vines. Then a flash, as of red and yellow lightning, consumes it all in an instant, and the blackened earth takes time to turn green again, as the rush and tumble begins to slow, and the uniform gray of the sky starts to flicker. At last he realizes he is watching night and day chase each other. The flickering slows further until at last day wins the chase, and he finds himself atop a bluff overlooking a vast ocean, with heather and wildflowers waving and nodding among gray stumps.

"See how good it is for plants to grow in the open air."

When the shepherd awakes, weary and marveling, only one coherent thought is able to form in his mind: "And there was evening and there was morning, the third day."

The shepherd awaits the approach of the next evening with something like dread. His mind is whirling with the swirling images of the night before, and he is exhausted from lack of untrammeled sleep.

When night falls, he finds himself on the same bluff. Nothing seems to have changed. There is wind, and heather, and an overcast sky.

From deep within the silence, your voice says, "Let there be lights in the dome of the sky to separate the day from the night; and let them be for signs and for seasons and for days and years, and let them be lights in the dome of the sky to give light upon the earth."

For the first time since the visions began, the sky begins to clear. To his left, the sun is setting in yellow and red. To his right, the full moon is rising, pendant and orange. Above, blue is pierced by the evening star. As blue deepens to purple, one by one more stars appear, with here and there a familiar constellation, if stretched and distorted. For hours he stares at the inscrutable sky, as the moon rises to its zenith.

"See how good it is to look beyond the sky."

The sky brightens suddenly, half the moon is gone, and he's back on the hillside with his sheep. Strangely, he feels rested and serene. The day passes slowly, full of thoughts he will never be able to put into words.

As the fifth evening approaches, he lays himself down a little apart from his sheep, fingers laced behind his head to look up at the panoplied heavens.

In the blink of an eye, he's on a wide beach, the bluff rising behind him. The voice says, "Let the waters bring forth swarms of living creatures, and let birds fly above the earth across the dome of the sky." The sun sinks too quickly upon his left, then rises upon his right in an instant, only to sink again, and rise, and sink, until it is a streak across the face of the firmament that wanders toward the south and then returns, ebbing and flowing like the waves of the sea, only to become a wide yellow stripe against a dim and star-streaked sky.

Around him the world thrums and throbs. He seems to be standing on an obsidian plain, as the bluff he had stood upon the night before recedes into the distance. For a time there is an eerie peace. Looking into the sky behind him he can see concentric circles, like those of a clay bowl. The striped dome is the only thing that maintains a motion of its own, as it wobbles ponderously, making him dizzy. He squeezes shut his eyes and waits, until a gentle breeze tugs at his beard and raucous cries assail his ears. When he looks, the sun has come to rest in a midmorning sky, and he is once again standing upon waves. The air is full of wheeling birds of a kind he has never seen. Some of them have teeth, and all are screaming and cawing.

Suddenly, one dives toward him. He throws his arms over his head and cowers, but a splash tells him he is not the bird's target. He glances up to see its orange tail feathers rising, a long fish dangling from its talons. Looking down at the clear water, he sees all manner of fish, of all sizes and shapes. Further down, a menacing shadow—some enormous, elongated beast with a neck like a serpent—undulates. A sudden urge to draw his feet up out of the water reveals a fact he hasn't noted before: His feet are planted as though invisible hands clasp his ankles. He is rescued from the edge of panic by another pronouncement: "Be fruitful and multiply and fill the waters in the seas, and let birds multiply on the earth." Your voice is strong and calm, the kind of voice the shepherd uses to quiet his sheep when an eagle circles overhead. He breathes deep and exhales through his mouth. At length the shadow passes, the fish subside, and the birds move away, following the creature who scares their prey toward the surface.

Your voice rings with exultation: "See how good it is to swim and fly."

This time the shepherd is relieved to be returned to his sheep, who are eager to move on to greener pastures.

He stumbles through that day, unable to shake his exhaustion. The sheep jostle him, sensing his agitation and wanting to stay close. By late afternoon he is miles away, with hardly the strength left to stand. He lies down beside a stream issuing from a narrow gorge cut into the foothills of the mountains.

When he awakes, he is already standing, and his sheep are gone. His first instinct is to run downstream in search of them, but his feet won't move. He is in the vision again, but this time, at first, the world seems unchanged. He's standing beside the same stream, in the same foothills, but the gorge—the gorge is much higher than it was when he fell asleep. A thin waterfall leaps from a crack in a high cliff and falls into a tiny pool.

Your now-familiar voice says: "Let the earth bring forth living creatures of every kind: cattle and creeping things and wild animals of the earth of every kind." The shepherd looks around but sees nothing but trees swaying gently in the wind. Presently a fox, or something nearly like a fox, walks to the stream and drinks. It's too big for a fox, and its coat is too dark, and yet the snout and ears and eyes are unmistakably foxy. When it lifts its head, the shepherd follows its gaze. More animals are stepping from the trees. A herd of tiny deer—perhaps gazelles—are cautiously approaching. Before the sun sets, the banks of the stream are crowded on both sides with a multitude of creatures coming and going, including a pride of great cats, a lone bear of enormous proportions, crowds of kine, wild ass and jackals, along with innumerable smaller beasts darting amongst the hooves and paws of the larger. The shepherd recognizes none of the specific breeds, but every type of animal he knows is there save one—the kind he loves most dearly.

Your voice says, "See how good it is to gather together at the time of the evening breeze."

As darkness deepens, the animals disperse. A gibbous moon tinges the muddied stream with silver. The shepherd wonders why the vision persists, since, ever before, the declaration of goodness has signalled the end of the dream.

At length, your voice speaks again: "Let us make humankind in our image, according to our likeness; and let them have dominion over the fish of the sea, and over the birds of the air, and over the cattle, and over all the wild animals of the earth, and over every creeping thing that creeps upon the earth."

The shepherd hears a whistle and turns. Striding upriver towards him is a tall woman draped in skins, bearing a staff. Behind her a herd of sturdy sheep are kept in tight formation by a circling dog. They pass close by without acknowledging his presence, then continue on and out of sight. With a pang of loneliness he realizes he hasn't talked to or even seen another human being since the day before these visions started.

The sound of voices returns his gaze downstream, where a band of people approach, appareled in crudely stitched skins. There are perhaps fifty, of all ages. In the midst of them walks an elderly man, bent of back but clear of eye, remarkable for the bear's skull he wears upon his head. Three long feathers, perhaps from an owl, dangle upon his shoulder. As the man draws even with the vision-locked shepherd, he pauses. With a grunt he reaches out a hand toward the shepherd's chest, then raises his arms and shouts.

The others gather around him, and he points to the shepherd's feet. He speaks words in a tongue unknown to the shepherd, and presently a couple of young boys draw near, bearing a largish rock between them, still dripping with river water. The old man directs them where to drop it. Soon more children approach, with more rocks, until the shepherd is enclosed within a miniature wall. Younger children bring sticks and brush, and pile them within the circle. The shepherd doesn't feel the branches that crisscross his shins, but when a woman kneels before him and opens a small shell amidst the fuel, the shepherd feels a thrill travel up his spine as flames begin to rise. He feels their warmth, but he does not find it uncomfortable.

Your voice, louder than the crackling flames and the chatter of the crowd (though they seem not to hear), says, "Be fruitful and multiply, and fill the earth and subdue it; and have dominion over the fish of the sea and over the birds of the air and over every living thing that moves upon the earth."

From his vantage point within the fire, the shepherd watches as the people set up a crude camp. Only one tent is erected, into which mothers with infants retire, along with a handful of other women. No cooking utensils are brought forth, but only baskets of woven reeds.

The voice says, "See, I have given you every plant yielding seed that is upon the face of all the earth, and every tree with seed in its fruit; you shall have them for food. And to every beast of the earth, and to every bird of the air, and to everything that creeps on the earth, everything that has the breath of life, I have given every green plant for food."

The people gather around the flame-engulfed shepherd; the baskets are opened and their contents distributed. Figs, pomegranates, apples, and dates, along with some kind of flatbread, are passed from hand to hand and eaten. When all have had their fill, the baskets are closed and set aside.

The old man stands and sings a guttural song, gesturing and hopping from foot to foot. The shepherd cannot see his face nor understand the words, but the melody tugs at deep longings in his heart, and when the old man leaps sideways, landing in a crouch with both hands raised in claws, the shepherd is as startled as everyone else. A little one starts to cry, but the old man tiptoes up and touches the child on the nose. The crying does not stop immediately, but as the old man stays crouched, his hand outstretched, the wailing falters, and the child takes his hand. Together they walk back toward the fire, and the elder continues his song, using the child as a prop, lifting and spinning until the child is giggling and all the people are roaring with laughter.

When the story is done, the people disperse, only to lie down together in unruly bunches not far from the fire. The old man alone remains awake, sitting cross-legged by the fire, rocking back and forth with his eyes closed and humming occasionally. With his crown of skull and feathers now at his side, his bald pate glows in the firelight. For a long time the shepherd can only stare in fascination, wondering what visions this old man might have seen, might be seeing even now. At length, the shepherd woman approaches, sits down beside him and slides one arm under his. Still humming and rocking, he puts his hand on hers.

Abruptly, his rocking stops, and the man sags against his companion, laying his head upon her shoulder. She reaches across to smooth the sparse hair from his brow. Then she speaks, and although the shepherd cannot understand the particulars, he comprehends the subject matter. She speaks of her sheep, the ones who are limping, or pregnant, or in conflict with another. When she is done, the man responds in kind, giving her news of the people, then singing snatches of his song, though softly, so as not to wake the others. He charades the child, the crying, the lifting and the laughter, until they both are laughing, struggling to keep their voices down, leaning into each other as they convulse with mirth.

"How great is that?" says your voice.

The shepherd awakes in darkness. The air has chilled, but his sheep have piled themselves around him to share each others' warmth. He feels certain that the visions of creation are now complete, though he hopes your voice may return from time to time. His heart is pierced with a deep pang at the thought that he will never again see the old man and the other shepherd. Watching them laugh together reminded him so much of his own wife, who long ago fell victim to Mother Eve's curse. He is as exhausted as he was when he lay down, but he struggles to his feet and lifts his hands to the sky, and tries to remember the old man's song.

When the sun rises he will take his flock back to the tents of his people. He will give his sheep into the care of his son, and he will sleep for a day and a night. And then he will call his grandson to him, and tell him the story of how the owner of the voice on the wind brought the whole world into being. The refrain he has already come up with will serve well to end the story:

"God saw everything that he had made, and indeed, it was very good. And there was evening and there was morning, the sixth day."

Chapter Two:
The Fall

Adam told Eve that even touching the Tree would be fatal, and this is the lie that unraveled paradise.

LET'S IMAGINE THAT ADAM AND EVE ACTUALLY existed, and that you put them in the garden of Eden for a purpose. I want to stress that this purpose, like the story about the shepherd's visions, is entirely made up. I have taken bits and pieces of knowledge and insight that have floated past me by chance, and I have built a plot around them. I have found this altered and augmented story helpful in clarifying my own ideas of who you are, and I hope the reader may find it so also, but, to the best of my knowledge, none of my alterations or additions have any basis in fact, not even the ones I now firmly believe.

The first such bit of knowledge is that the word *paradise* derives from the Old Persian **paridayda-*, meaning "walled enclosure." Now, this word was not associated with the Hebrew phrase translated as "the garden of Eden" until much later, when the Septuagint translated it with the Greek word *paradaisos* (παράδεισος). This factoid added little to my understanding of the story until I came across a theory regarding Noah's flood, wherein a glacier that was damming up the Black Sea broke apart precipitously, inundating the Fertile Crescent. The theory is not widely accepted, but the two ideas sparked a possibility that intrigued me:

What if you wanted Adam and Eve to build a breakwater around Eden, enclosing thousands if not millions of acres that would otherwise be swept away, thereby protecting any number of unique and precious plants and animals, including, I speciously surmise, a couple of trees that could withstand years of drought while still producing life-sustaining fruit? Adam and Eve had more than 1500 years to build it before the deluge arrived, if the genealogical timeline is an accurate gauge, and help would arrive with their children, but unfortunately, due to circumstances entirely within their control, they never got a chance to begin.

The first to be brought to the garden was Adam, who naturally would assume you formed him specially out of dust, since he had no conscious memory of his parents, gave little thought to the significance of his belly button, and would remember you saying later that from dust he had come and to dust he would one day return. In reality, though (or at least in the reality I'm currently making up), he was a foundling Neanderthal child.

Perhaps his parents died, perhaps they abandoned him, or perhaps he wandered away from his family and got lost. Maybe he was literally the last of his kind. In any event, he felt lonely and forsaken, and you identified with him, and you accepted responsibility for him, and so you (or anyway someone who identified with you and thus was you incarnate) took it upon yourself to lead him to a little niche that was protected from the elements, free from predators, and had nearly an endless supply of easily accessible fruit. It was a special place, where grew trees that could be found nowhere else. One tree in particular was the first of its kind, and it was risky to let a human being loose within sight of it, especially such a young one, but you sternly enjoined Adam not to eat of that tree, on pain of death. Being but a child, Adam understandably developed a superstitious dread of this tree that was perhaps more extreme than was strictly warranted, but it was an important tree, and not for children to eat from willy-nilly.

Adam had a peculiar rapport with animals and a talent for taming them. He tamed canines and felines, equines and ovines, birds and reptiles, rodents and spiders, but none of them brought an end to his loneliness.

Then one day he awoke to find a human being staring down at him, and his heart performed a series of backflips.

Silly to think you created her special from one of his ribs, but what other explanation did he have at his disposal? So what if maybe the pain in his side came from this new human being kicking him awake? And what did it matter? Here at last was someone who could talk back, with whom he could explore and laugh and play. Here was poetry and a cure for all loneliness. Where she truly came from, who can say? You brought these two human beings together because they needed each other. And, according to my theory, you needed them.

One of the first things Adam did, as he was showing her around the place, was to warn the woman how dangerous was the fruit of that one tree. To impress upon her the severity of the ban, he added one tiny lie: that even to touch its bark would bring instant death.

For all we know, your command was meant only for Adam the child, lest he devour every fruit from the tree every year, effectively sterilizing it, but now that he was older, perhaps the species' population was well-established. It's even possible that the fruit was poisonous, but only until it was fully ripened, or that it had psychotropic properties that could have damaged an adolescent's brain. Perhaps, had they asked, you would now have allowed them to eat of its wonderful fruit.

Regardless, the man never thought to ask such a thing, and, one day, as they were walking past it, the woman noticed a snake slithering among its branches. She could hardly help notice it betrayed no sign of dying.

Now, the word *serpent* can signify anything from a worm to a dragon, so it may be that what she saw was a worm poking its head from the side of a fruit, or perhaps it was a dragon who audibly spoke to her. I'm going to assume (for the moment at least) that it was a normal, garden-variety, speechless snake, in which case, the snake's immunity to the deadly tree was all it took to pursuade Eve to question Adam's report of your injunction. She reached out her hand, plucked a fruit, and took a bite. *Oh, I bet it was good.* In an instant she went from wishing to prove the man wrong to wanting to share this amazing fruit with him.

Adam's reaction is lost to us. Genesis records only that he was standing beside her, and that he took what she handed him and ate.

Now, the serpent may have been the larva of a codling moth, it may have been a simple, mute, garden snake, or it may have been a dragon, or Satan himself.

The Hebrew word for Satan is הַשָּׂטָן (ha-Satan), which means "the accuser." He was not created evil. You, who identify so closely with your creatures, are sometimes blind to our flaws, so you need an accuser to help you see clearly. The English word *dragon* comes from Greek δράκων (*drákōn*), "dragon, serpent of huge size, water-snake," which possibly comes from the verb δρακεῖν (*drakeîn*) "to see clearly." (Take all this with a Wikipedian grain of salt.)

So, the serpent, even if a clear-eyed, satanic dragon, was just doing its job by testing whether Adam and Eve were worthy of continued survival.

"Then the eyes of both were opened, and they knew that they were naked."

To be naked is to be vulnerable, and you glory in vulnerability, because to be vulnerable is to be trusting entirely in you. In truth, they were more vulnerable at this moment than they had ever been before, because their continued existence, not just individually but as a species, was in jeopardy.

Realizing this, their first instinct was to hide their reproductive organs behind fig leaves. When they heard you coming, they attempted to hide their whole selves.

I imagine them hiding behind slender trees, like children secreted behind the couch with their feet sticking out.

At first you were thinking, *Have they invented a new game?* You asked, "Where are you?" The man answered, "I heard the sound of you in the garden, and I was afraid, because I was naked; and I hid myself."

Uh-oh, was your second thought. "Who told you that you were naked? Have you eaten from the tree of which I commanded you not to eat?"

How your heart must have sunk at Adam's reply: "The woman whom you gave to be with me, she gave me fruit from the tree, and I ate." The smug smile on the serpent's face didn't help matters, but though "the serpent was more crafty than any other wild animal that the Lord God had made," Adam was craftier still. It pierced your heart to see how easily the man took on the accusational nature of the serpent. He was basically saying, *Since you gave me the woman, you also, by extension, gave me the fruit that she handed me. If my trespass isn't the woman's fault, then it must be yours. It certainly isn't mine!*

The Fall of Man did not occur through disobedience or the consumption of a piece of fruit. It happened right here when Adam failed to accept responsibility for his own action.

You accept responsibility for everything, and you wanted Adam to do likewise—to emulate you—but he had chosen the serpent's way instead. Rather than faulting his logic, you turned to Eve. "What is this that you have done?"

She, too, had the opportunity to identify with you by accepting responsibility for her actions, but she chose instead to follow the man's lead, saying, "The serpent tricked me, and I ate."

Both of them were telling the truth, but they were speaking in the language of the serpent, who has a forked tongue, allowing them to say two things at once: *Yes, I ate it, and it wasn't my fault.* Had they been speaking your language, the man might have said, "I lied to the woman, telling her that even to touch the tree meant certain death. She saw through the lie, and she ate, and then I, in my foolishness, ate also," and the woman could have said, "I listened to the voice of the serpent instead of trusting the voice of my husband, who was speaking the very words of God for my benefit, and I ate, and furthermore, I gave the fruit to the man." Who knows, perhaps you would have followed such admissions with a confession of your own—that you would never have killed Adam simply for eating a piece of fruit. You all could have had a good laugh at your mutual misunderstandings, and Adam and Eve might still be alive in their garden today.

But there's another possibility worth noting, something else that Eve truthfully could have said but did not. She could have said, "The man lied to me, combining a truth and a falsehood, so that I was defenseless against the half-truths of the serpent." But instead of retaliating with a good old-fashioned "He started it!" and shifting the blame back to Adam (or to you), she adopted his tactic but deflected the blame in the only direction it could truly be shared. So, even though she didn't accept full responsibility for eating the fruit in the first place, she accepted Adam's accusation, and thus accepted responsibility for her part in his actions.

I imagine there were tears streaming down your face as you turned at last to the serpent, who was trying, I further imagine, to don a seriouser demeanor, but you had no further questions.

You said, "Because you have done this, cursed are you among all animals and among all wild creatures; upon your belly you shall go, and dust you shall eat all the days of your life. I will put enmity between you and the woman, and between your offspring and hers; he will strike your head, and you will strike his heel."

Whatever remained of the serpent's smile was vanished now, its victory turned to ashes. Had it expected praise for revealing the flaw in human nature, ensuring that their offspring would be cut off before it was too late, before, say, humans could grow powerful enough to cause an extinction-level event all on their own? But the job of the accuser is to accuse, not to tempt, and not to judge. Thus the serpent overreached, to its own detriment.

The first component of the curse lends support to the idea that the serpent was a dragon, and that it and/or its offspring would now be stripped of leg and wing. The second component revealed that the woman's offspring would not be cut off, meaning the serpent had just made a formidable enemy.

To the woman you said, "I will greatly increase your pangs in childbearing; in pain you shall bring forth children, yet your desire shall be for your husband, and he shall rule over you." This was not so much a curse as a consequence, as surely as the coming flood was a simple consequence of the receding ice age. You accept responsibility for everything, and so you accepted responsibility for the woman's increased pain, just as you accepted responsibility for the animosity between the woman's offspring and the serpent's, even though you were the direct cause of neither. Childbirth is painful enough, but fear and anxiety (so I'm told) make it all the worse. You saw that the woman's heart was toward the man, and would be all the more so now that the man was about to be handicapped by his own set of curses, but the man would continue to blame her, to attempt to dominate her, and her fear and anxiety would only increase.

But the doom you needed to pronounce upon the man was the most heart-wrenching of all, for, under his curse, the whole world would suffer.

You said to the man, "Because you have listened to the voice of your wife, and have eaten of the tree about which I commanded you, 'You shall not eat of it,' cursed is the ground because of you; in toil you shall eat of it all the days of your life; thorns and thistles it shall bring forth for you; and you shall eat the plants of the field. By the sweat of your face you shall eat bread until you return to the ground, for out of it you were taken; you are dust, and to dust you shall return."

In other words, your threats are never idle. On the day Adam ate of the fruit of the knowledge of Good and Evil, his patriarchal lineage was doomed to peter out. Eve's line would continue through Sarah, Rebekah, and Leah to Judah, a man not of Adam's line who would ultimately pass the test that Adam failed.

[If it seems to you, dear reader, that the story of these women is tangential to the biblical narrative, and that Judah was clearly of the line of Adam, I would submit that that's because the story was told (and Genesis was written) by men, some of whom outright lied. The fact that the matriarchal thread is still visible to those with eyes to see is testament to the power of divine inspiration.]

But we'll get to all that later.

The final curse was eviction from the garden, but that too was more consequence than curse, for the expulsion happened the moment they stopped believing you to be good. Since they no longer trusted you to provide, they would have to find some way to trust in themselves. They would need to raise crops and store up food instead of eating what was available on any given day. And they would no longer have any time to walk with you.

As for their nudity—It had been their glory, symbolizing their vulnerability and, thus, their complete dependence on you, for they were naked even in comparison to other animals. Alas, the world was now against them, and fig leaves were not going to cut it. You knew that they would start to follow the practices of other humans and kill animals to cover their nakedness—still hoping to protect their reproductive organs from a hostile world, so you accepted responsibility even for this, to the point that you were willing to make their first garments yourself.

In writing this chapter, I spent an inordinate amount of time wondering what kind of animal provided their skins. A woolly mammoth? A unicorn? A saber-toothed tiger? Any of these animals could symbolically represent species that have gone extinct due to human activity, either through overhunting or destruction of habitat. Perhaps, if humanity had proven ourselves responsible, and accepted our responsibility as custodians, any or all of these species would still be with us today.

But no, it makes the most sense to me that the animal you sacrificed to make their clothes was a sheep. I don't know what it is with you and sheep, but it appears that they exemplify some quality you highly prize. Perhaps it's their vulnerability, or their stupidity, or some other trait that they share with human beings.

I assume you were weeping as you beckoned the sheep and watched it trustingly present itself to your blade. While you slit its throat, gutted and skinned it, stretched and dried its skin to be stitched into garments, the human couple watched, learning how it was done. Rather than grieving along with you, Adam was trying to patch things up with his wife, calling her Eve, which means "living." Genesis says "the mother of all living." I imagine he was saying, "Well, it turned out all right in the end—I guess we *do* get to keep on living." Eve, I imagine, was weeping with you for the life of the sheep.

Your goal with *Homo sapiens sapiens* was a species of primate who loved even as you love. You chose this particular man and this particular woman to be the custodians of the world, to reign over creation in the same way that you reign, which is to say, not from a position of power and authority but from a posture of humility and compassion. You wanted to partner with them, so that they would share your responsibilities, much as Satan and the other angels did, with everyone working together to bless the world and its inhabitants.

But alas the blessing had turned to a curse, and because you identify so completely with your creation, all four curses applied equally to you. Your ability to judge was now hampered by the disabilities of the serpent. The task of giving birth to a new creation would be as painful for you as for the woman. As the earth was cursed to the man, so was the man cursed to you, sprouting thorns and thistles where you had hoped to grow good fruit. And Adam and Eve's eviction from your garden was equally your eviction from them.

Almost it would seem better to scrap the whole project and start over, to accept the serpent's judgement and declare humanity unworthy of continued investment, but you glory in vulnerability, and so you chose to risk the entire planetary ecosystem on the flimsy hope that the human project could yet be redeemed.

The rest of Genesis (indeed, the rest of the Hebrew scriptures) is the story of your quest for a few good men. Your focus was on men because men are the problem. Not because women are pure beings who never sin, but because motherhood was not irreparably damaged by the Fall, whereas fatherhood was pretty much annihilated. Indeed, the reason you identify yourself as Father is in order to show men how it's done. Ultimately, you were hoping to find a man whom you could claim as your only-begotten son. Someone who would identify with you as completely as you identify with each of us.

The company of the woman was your greatest gift to the man. The man's blaming of her for a disobedience that belonged to him alone, and her acceptance of that blame has, I dare say, been the fate of many a relationship since. As for Adam and Eve themselves—aside from a few acts of procreation, they are never mentioned in Genesis again. Having proven unwilling to accept responsibility for themselves, I doubt they took much responsibility for raising their children.

Their firstborn son was Cain. When Cain grew up, he became a farmer. In other words, he participated in his father's curse and tilled the soil by the sweat of his brow. His younger brother Abel, by contrast, was a shepherd. In other words, while Cain was hard at work doing his duty, even (may it be said) taking responsibility, Abel was ignoring his father's curse and gadding about with a flock of sheep. Is it any wonder Cain was angry when you had regard for Abel's offering from the flock but no regard for his own offering from the field?

It may well be that Abel was eating bread from Cain's grain. In fact, Cain's harvest may have been feeding the entire family, yet, whenever Abel sacrificed one of his precious sheep for a feast, their parents were jubilant, all the while eating Cain's daily bread with nothing more than a grunt and a nod.

To have you react the same way was simply too much. Cain's jaw dropped, and he held out his arms in the universal gesture that means, "You have got to be kidding me!"

You saw his reaction, and said to him, "Why are you angry, and why has your countenance fallen? If you do well, will you not be accepted? And if you do not do well, sin is lurking at the door; its desire is for you, but you must master it."

Your disregard for Cain's offering was not a rejection of him. You loved Cain, and identified with him, and furthermore, intended to bless him with a family and long life. You had regard for Abel's offering not because you were playing favorites, but because you saw in Abel the more likely ancestor of the redeemer you sought. The difference was simply that Cain accepted the curse while Abel did not. I can't say definitively that you prefer the nomadic life of animal husbandry to the more rooted occupation of agriculture, but I am quite sure you intended your eventually-begotten son to be a curse breaker, not a curse keeper.

Alas, Cain's wrath was not to be turned away by a simple pep talk. He invited Abel out to a field, rose up against him, and killed him. *Now*, he thought, *God and my parents will have no choice but to have regard for Cain.*

When you saw the look on his face you asked, "Where is your brother Abel?"

He said, "I do not know; am I my brother's keeper?"

No, he was not, and he thereby confirmed that he was no better at accepting responsibility than his father.

You said, "What have you done? Listen; your brother's blood is crying out to me from the ground! And now you are cursed from the ground, which has opened its mouth to receive your brother's blood from your hand. When you till the ground, it will no longer yield to you its strength; you will be a fugitive and a wanderer on the earth."

This curse, like the ones pronounced upon his parents, the serpent, and the very ground, was merely an unavoidable consequence. You were revealing what Cain would discover for himself soon enough: that he would no longer be able to till the ground without seeing his brother's blood spilling upon it. He would be a fugitive and a wanderer because he would no longer be able to look his mother and father in the face. You pronounced it as a curse because, as I keep saying, you accept responsibility for everything.

Cain did not yet understand any of that. He said, "My punishment is greater than I can bear! Today you have driven me away from the soil, and I shall be hidden from your face; I shall be a fugitive and a wanderer on the earth, and anyone who meets me may kill me."

As grief-stricken as you were at the death of Abel and all those whom Abel might have sired, your compassion now was for Cain, for the life that he would have to live, bereft not only of his brother but of everything he had ever known. You acknowledged the truth of his words and replied, "Not so! Whoever kills Cain will suffer a sevenfold vengeance." Whatever kind of mark it was that you placed upon his head to serve as a warning to others, you inscribed it with great care. Perhaps you seared it into his forehead with your own burning tears.

As for Abel, I don't want to move on without acknowledging that he did the right thing when his brother rose up against him: He accepted his vulnerability and he died. For this reason alone, he would have been a worthy ancestor of the coming redeemer.

The long winter of the previous ice age was ending, and an epic spring was about to begin, but the meltwaters were going to destroy your garden and everyone in it. Your plan for dealing with the flood had been to place a couple of human beings in the garden and, over the course of generations—hundreds of years—you would lead them and their descendants in the building of a dike, a sea wall that would divert the flood to either side, along the Euphrates to the west, along the Tigris on the east. It would have been the world's first arboretum and wildlife preserve, where anyone who wanted could come and be saved.

Good God, it would have been fun! All the preparation, all the sideways glances from those who would assume that the clan of Adam and Eve were touched. "Why are you building the walls so high?" they would have asked. "Are you expecting to be attacked by giants?" How they would have shaken their heads at talk of a future flood.

And then their looks of wonder and terror when the waters began to rise and they rushed into Eden, where the gates were wide and welcoming, and the story of Adam and Eve's hospitality would be told for hundreds of thousands of years.

Alas, Adam and Eve had proven themselves unfit for the job, as had Cain and, *oh, your dear Abel!* But there was still time. Centuries, in fact. Eden was ideally situated, but there were other places, other solutions, other opportunities. All you needed were a few good people who would listen to your voice, believe what you were telling them, and accept responsibility for the project.

Centuries passed, generation after generation of no one willing to listen. Many cried, "Lord, Lord!" but no one gave heed to your voice. Surrounded by adoring angels, and a host of humans crying out your name, you felt lonely and forsaken.

But you would not give up hope.

At last, Enoch, son of Jared, son of Mahalalel, son of Kenan, son of Enosh, son of Seth the third son of Eve, took heed and listened to your voice. He walked with you as Adam and Eve had walked with you in the beginning. Together you and he talked for hours, and days, even centuries, about everything under the sun, but particularly working together to come up with a solution to the problem of the imminent flood. It was too late now to build a wall around the garden. It was too late to save the majority of people and animals, but, between the two of you, a plan was taking shape that could save a few, if any would listen.

By now the ground was so saturated with violent blood that the earth itself was crying out to you in agony. By now an unabated flood would be a blessing, cleansing the earth of its curse, whose name was humanity.

Now Enoch loved his grandson above everyone else. Indeed, it may have been Enoch to whom you revealed the outline of creation. He begged you to hold back the flood until his grandson Lamech could die a natural death. You agreed, though it would cost you an untold price, and then led him to a distant land, where he could learn how ships are made, so that when he returned he could stand in for you (just as someone else had stood in for you with Adam and Eve in the times of the evening breeze), and give specific instructions to his great grandson. Whether that as-yet-unborn person would act upon those instructions remained to be seen, but Enoch *as Enoch* was never seen by his people again.

Chapter Three:
The Winter

Father Abraham told many lies.

Noah built an ark, gathered two of every kind, survived the flood, saw a rainbow, and lived happily ever after. Right?

After they disembarked, you blessed Noah and his family as if it were Chapter One all over again, telling them to be fruitful and multiply, and Noah, as always, did exactly as he was told: He got drunk on grape wine and had a roll in the hay with his wife.

His wife, strangely, is never named, and after getting on the ark in the first place is never mentioned again except obliquely. The story says, "He drank some of the wine and became drunk, and he lay uncovered in his tent. And Ham, the father of Canaan, saw the nakedness of his father." According to Leviticus 18:7, "You shall not uncover the nakedness of your father, which is the nakedness of your mother." Therefore I'm going to assume that Ham saw both his parents lying naked in their tent.

It's an odd bit of story, and I'm surely missing important aspects of it, but Ham went and told his brothers what he saw, and here is one of many places in Scripture where a little more novelistic detail might paint a clearer picture. I mean, supposedly all three brothers were married at this point (in fact, Shem is 98), and yet Ham I picture as a twelve- or thirteen-year-old boy, eyes wide and mouth covered as though he's just seen his first porno mag (remember, they didn't have the internet back then), and he invites his brothers to come see for themselves. His brothers respond by walking a garment backward into the tent and covering the nakedness of their parents without looking upon them.

When Noah awoke from his stupor, he was some upset, and had words for his sons. Ham he cursed to be the slave of his brothers. Japheth he blessed that God would make room for him amongst his big brother Shem's tents. Shem he just outright blessed to high heaven.

It seems significant that Noah was taking on one of your characteristics, pronouncing blessings and curses upon his sons in just the way that Adam apparently never did. I'm not saying he did a good job of it, but it seems like a step in the right direction.

But here's the thing: Genesis was written by a Semitic people (Shemites), so the curse that Noah pronounced upon the father of the Canaanites seems conveniently favorable for descendents of Shem living in a Promised Land after forcibly displacing the previous occupants who—oh yeah—just happened to be Canaanites. Or perhaps that's too cynical. Maybe God chose to ratify the blessings pronounced by Noah, and the curse as well. But my imagination is unequal to the task of seeing how these blessings and this curse compare to the consequences you pronounced in Eden. Unless...

Unless the consequences came, not as a result of the actions of his sons, but as a simple result of Noah's pronouncements. Yes, parents have such power. Shame on Ham and glory to Shem and Japheth, passed down father to son from generation to generation.

After the flood, people started building cities. With the curse on the ground washed away, agriculture took off, and urban areas could be fed without the need for individual inhabitants to contribute any sweat from their own brows. This gave them leisure to turn their minds to other things. In a city called Babel they decided to build a tower to the heavens.

Nothing wrong with a tower, one might think, but towers are closely followed by slums, and you weren't ready to deal with slums just yet. So you brought down their tower, perhaps with an earthquake, perhaps with a well-placed breeze, and then you scattered them and confused their language. How? I don't know. Probably over the course of generations. You seem rarely to do things instantaneously.

The slums would come, in time, along with all the other problems that cities create. Cut off from the soil that sustains them, people tend to forget about earth, and forget about you, and turn instead to business, politics, and organized religion.

God help us all.

According to the biblical timeline, Noah was still alive when his great-great-great-great-great-great-great-grandson Abram (who would later be called Abraham) was begat by Terah in a place called Ur. Abram had two brothers: Nahor and Haran. And here's where things get unnecessarily confusing:

> Now these are the descendants of Terah. Terah was the father of Abram, Nahor, and Haran; and Haran was the father of Lot. Haran died before his father Terah in the land of his birth, in Ur of the Chaldeans. Abram and Nahor took wives; the name of Abram's wife was Sarai, and the name of Nahor's wife was Milcah. She was the daughter of Haran the father of Milcah and Iscah. Now Sarai was barren; she had no child.

Notice that the first Haran mentioned is Terah's son, the father of Lot, and that the second Haran is described simply as the father of Milcah and Iscah, with no other clues as to how or if he was related. The name Iscah appears nowhere else in the Bible, but she's considered by some to be Sarai (later Sarah), the sister of Milcah and Lot, (or even the sister of Milcah and the aunt of Lot).

Considering how keen the Bible is on genealogies, the blurring of relationships here is striking. Abraham later claims that Sarah is his father's daughter by a different mother (which by the customs of the day could truthfully be said were she either his father's daughter or granddaughter). So who is Sarai? The word means "princess," so it's possible that it was only Abraham's pet name for her. Allow me to suggest that the relationships have been deliberately obscured in order to hide in plain sight the "shocking" and "hilarious" lie concerning the "children of Abraham."

Genesis would have us believe that Sarah was only ten years younger than Abraham, and thus well past menopause when she gave birth miraculously to Isaac. But if in fact Sarah was Iscah and Iscah was the sister of Lot, then, from what I understand of the customs of the time, Abram and Nahor would have become as fathers to all three of their brother Haran's children after he died. Instead, according to my theory, they married their nieces, who were in fact much, much younger than them.

Now, Abram was 75 years old when you told him to leave his father's house and continue on to the area that in later years would be called the Promised Land. Had you given Terah the same instructions? Genesis doesn't say, but it's possible that you had asked every male descendent of Noah to leave the city of the Chaldeans and head to the land of Ham's descendants, and that only Abram had fully heeded the call, so you told him that he would become a mighty nation, and that all who blessed him would be blessed, and all who cursed him would be cursed.

Unfortunately, when he arrived, there was a famine in the land, and what do you mean, "there was a famine in the land"? This is where you told him to go, and here he is, and you're telling him there's nothing here to eat?

Perhaps Abraham and his household were supposed to fast like Jesus in the wilderness and trust you to provide, understanding that man does not live by bread alone. And so, perhaps, he failed you in retreating to Egypt, back to the urban environment you were trying to get him to leave, or perhaps those two Edenic tree species destroyed in the flood were supposed to prevent famines, but they were extinct by this point, so . . . Welcome to life in a fallen world, I guess?

In Egypt, Abram told Sarai her beauty was liable to get him killed. He asked her to accept a demotion to sister in the eyes of anyone who asked, the immediate result of which was to allow Pharaoh to take her as his wife, which he did. Coincidentally, Pharaoh treated Abram well, because that's how the brothers of beautiful women were treated back then. However, once Pharaoh figured out the reason for the inexplicable plagues that beset his household, he upbraided Abram for not taking responsibility for Sarai *as his wife* and sent him on his way.

By the time they got back to the Negeb, the flocks and families of Abram and Lot were becoming too numerous to peaceably coexist, so Abram let Lot choose in which direction he wanted to take his flocks and family, and offered to take his own flocks and family in the other direction. Unsurprisingly, Lot opted for the richer land (the valley that contained the cities of Sodom and Gomorrah), while Abram contentedly went the other way.

Does it seem odd to you that while Abram seemed perfectly happy to let Pharaoh take Sarai, as soon as Lot was captured by a local king, Abram pursued the king with a small army and rescued him? I mean, maybe it was the times, maybe that's what was expected of men back then, but it seems odd to me. Since it happens twice each (that he shows more concern for his nephew than his wife), it seems reasonable to infer that the text is intentionally underlining the oddity.

You credited it to him as righteousness that Abram believed you that his heir would be a son of his own loins, and that his descendants would be as numerous as the stars, but what did you credit to him when he listened to Sarai suggesting that they take matters into their own hands and have

Abram go into Hagar, her Egyptian slave? The text doesn't say. Nor does it offer any hint of your reaction when Hagar cast a contemptuous eye upon her mistress for successfully conceiving, and Sarai, enraged, turned to Abram and said, "May the wrong done to me be on you!"

I suppose we are meant to assume that such is the life that Adam and Eve prepared for their descendants. By now you were in the business of blessing even their mistakes, and so you promised to make a mighty nation out of Hagar's son Ishmael as well, even though he was not, apparently, the one promised.

Finally, when Abram was 99 years old, you made a new covenant with him, changed his name to Abraham, meaning "father of multitudes," and instituted the practice of male circumcision (the point of which, I would suggest, was to make men *more* naked, *more* vulnerable in spite of their clothing). Then you told Abraham to stop calling his wife Sarai (*a* princess) and to call her Sarah (*the* princess). In other words, you ordered him to start taking his pet name for her seriously and in fact to acknowledge her as his superior. Both of these semantic changes involved simply adding the Hebrew letter *heh* to each of their names.

"Heh." Seriously?

You added a laugh to Sarai and Abram's name, then proceeded to tell Abraham that Sarah would bear a child the following year, at which point he fell on his face and lived up to the addition to his name by chuckling. Then he said to you, "O that Ishmael might live in your sight!" You had been promising him a son his entire life, and now he had one. His barren wife was well past the child-bearing age, so obviously this was some sort of deep theological joke. You responded by telling him to name his son Isaac, which means "he will laugh."

Later, after every man in Abraham's household had been circumcised, you showed up with a couple of buddies on your way to see for yourself whether Sodom and Gomorrah were as rotten as you had heard. Sarah was listening at the tent flap when you repeated your promise that she would bear a son in due season. She too lived up to her new name and laughed to herself, apparently at the mere thought of she and Abraham having sex, let alone of her getting pregnant as a result.

You said to Abraham, "Why did Sarah laugh, and say, 'Shall I indeed bear a child, now that I am old?' Is anything too wonderful for the Lord? At the set time I will return to you, in due season, and Sarah shall have a son."

The reason you didn't address Sarah directly is that the question wasn't meant for her. You were saying to Abraham, "What, you didn't even tell her what I already told you?"

Sarah, however, assumed the question was indirectly addressed to her, and said, "I did not laugh."

Then you addressed her directly and said, "Oh yes, you did laugh."

When you told Abraham your plans for Sodom and Gomorrah, he immediately started telling you how unjust it would be for you to destroy all of Sodom if fifty righteous people were living in the city. You assured him that, for the sake of fifty, you would spare the whole place. Considering all he knew about the city, doubt crept into Abraham's heart, and he said, "What if Sodom were five righteous people short of fifty?" You assured him that for the sake of forty-five, you would not destroy the city. Abraham was starting to see the problem with Sodom. "What if there are only forty, thirty, twenty, or ten?" You assured him that ten righteous people would suffice to safeguard the entire city, but Abraham wasn't actually concerned for the inhabitants of Sodom (as evidenced by the fact that he spoke not a word on behalf of Gomorrah): Sodom was the home of his nephew Lot.

I had always assumed that Lot was one (perhaps the only) righteous person in Sodom. I don't know why. There's no canonical evidence to support that assumption. In the end, Lot and his wife and daughters had to be forcibly removed from Sodom, since they wouldn't willingly leave. They were told to escape to the hills and not look back, but Lot was afraid the destruction would overtake them there, so he asked whether they could escape to that little city over there, instead. You agreed, and even conceded that you would spare that little city on Lot's behalf.

Maybe I'm reading my own bias into the biblical text, but I detect a preference, on your part, for wilderness over urban living. Abraham left the city of Haran and set out for the wilderness, Lot along with him, but it appears to me that Lot had decided that "roughing it" was not to his liking.

You waited until Lot reached the little city before raining fire and brimstone upon the big cities, and Lot's wife, behind him, turned to look upon Sodom's destruction and was transformed into a pillar of salt.

Let me ask you something: who else in all the Bible was ever transformed into something inhuman, let alone inanimate? I don't pretend to know what *really* happened to her, but I suspect that Lot did not deserve to escape your wrath. I think the fire and the brimstone raining from the sky formed pillars of salt, and whenever people asked what had happened to his wife he'd say, "Oh, her? Yeah, um, she was turned into a pillar of salt? such as you see in the valley of Sodom? because she disobeyed the angels of the Lord by looking back upon the destruction of Sodom. Yeah. So sad."

I likewise find suspect the story of his daughters getting him drunk and sleeping with him in order that they might bear descendants for their father. I mean, I get that in those days women without male relatives were considerably less secure than such women would be today, and that Lot's daughters had good reason to believe the world was ending and that they would need male replacements for when their father inevitably died, but Genesis makes it very clear that Lot didn't remember having sex with either daughter. But here's the thing: being blackout drunk is not conducive to a stiff erection. What I strongly suspect is that Lot got drunk and raped his daughters, probably more than once, and afterwards blamed them for getting pregnant. Like Adam, like Cain, he was unwilling to accept responsibility for his own heinous actions. This was a man, remember, who was willing to offer his wife and daughters to the crowd of men who wanted to become better acquainted (in a violently "biblical" way) with the angels Lot had taken in as guests.

He was not a good man. Certainly he was not a good father. I don't care what the ancient customs of hospitality demanded.

Anyone keeping track will notice that this is the first time I've accused the Bible not just of myth, misdirection, or deliberate obfuscation, but of an outright lie. I don't do so lightly, but for the sake of those who revere the Bible as a holy and wholly honest tome, I offer this question: what if we're *meant* to see through Lot's lie? What if, having seen that men in Genesis have a habit of not accepting responsibility for their actions, we're supposed to be able to see through their lies without being explicitly told, not only in the Bible, but also in our daily lives, where seemingly good-hearted men still lie and refuse to accept responsibility?

You saved Lot to honor Abraham, but in saving him, didn't you also fail to save his daughters from his lust? I think you did, but even if you didn't, you still accepted responsibility for the outcome. You couldn't stop Lot's crime, and the children of those awful unions, Moab and Ammon, begat tribes who would be notorious enemies of Israel. And then, out of nowhere, a whole book of the Bible is dedicated to a Moabite named Ruth, famous for being the great-grandmother of King David and, by extension, of your son Jesus.

Of course, the implication of Lot's lie being presented as truth (I'm sure no one asked Lot's daughters to verify his story) leads inexorably to calling shenanigans on Abraham himself.

Immediately after Sodom's destruction and just before Isaac's birth, there's another instance recorded of Abraham and Sarah claiming to be siblings and of a king taking her to be his wife.

But hold on a second—Sarah is 90 years old when King Abimelech adds her to his harem. Okay, so the patriarchs lived longer than modern people. I can accept that, and even without any superhuman vitality, 90-year-old women have a beauty all their own, right? But Genesis is pretty clear that Sarah had been through menopause, so why take her as a wife?

Okay, so maybe Abimelech had a thing for older women, but what if, as I earlier surmised, she was not Abraham's cousin or half-sister but his niece, considerably younger than 90, and not really postmenopausal? What if these were lies told to Isaac later on, in order to spare him the more sordid truth? What if Sarah was never really barren at all, but Abraham refused to accept responsibility for his own sterility or perhaps even his disinterest in women. What if—as suddenly seems incredibly likely and, again, as though we're *meant* to see it—Sarah was impregnated by King Abimelech?

You might argue that Abraham had been perfectly virile when he got Hagar pregnant, but who knows who else might have been sleeping with her at the time? What if she came to Sarah (then Sarai) distraught, told her that she was pregnant, and Sarai had had the brilliant, selfless idea of suggesting that Abraham (then Abram) sleep with the poor girl before her pregnancy started to show, allowing her to avoid the shame of unwed pregnancy while simultaneously giving Abram the heir for whom he had so long waited?

If I'm right, then the line of Adam died with Abraham. The "father of multitudes" died childless, and you were right to say that the one who would strike the head of the offspring of the serpent would be the offspring of Eve (not Adam).

If I am revealing Abraham's shame, I hope I am also unveiling a bit of Sarah's glory. She always struck me as something of a bee-eye-tee-see-aitch in regard to Hagar and Ishmael, especially considering the whole affair had been her idea. But imagine if my speculation is correct—that Hagar was pregnant out of wedlock and Sarah did her an extravagant favor by tricking Abraham into thinking the child was his: Suddenly, Hagar's contemptuous eye seems a lot more contemptible.

But this hypothesis also makes more sense of the angel's injunction to Hagar to return and submit to her mistress. I used to hate the idea of you telling her to return to an abusive relationship, but thirteen years later, Hagar and Ishmael were still with them, so I have some hope that Hagar's submission softened Sarah's heart, and that she treated her better after her return, but once Sarah gave birth to a healthy baby boy of her own, I can imagine she was heartily regretting her thirteen-year-old ruse.

She was in a bind. She was no doubt angry with Abraham for being so dense that he couldn't figure things out on his own, but she would hardly want him to grow a brain now, lest he realize the truth of Isaac's paternity. But to have a child that was no relation to either one of them be heir to her husband's wealth and legacy was devastating now that she had a child of her own.

Had Abraham really been the father of Ishmael, then Sarah would not have been justified in wanting her son to be the heir, since the customs of the day were clearly in favor of the birthright going to the eldest male child of the father (or at least, they would be by the time of Deuteronomy 21:15, and assuming Hagar would qualify as his wife, which it would seem she would). But in any event, it's certainly understandable that Sarah would hate the thought of her slave's child inheriting what her own child would not, and if Ishmael wasn't really Abraham's either, then her desire that Hagar and her son be banished is also suddenly more understandable (though still harsh).

Abraham wanted to protest, but you told him essentially the same thing you told Hagar: "whatever Sarah says to you, do as she tells you."

Abraham didn't understand, but (perhaps touchingly) he obeyed. He loaded Hagar with a waterskin and sent her and the thirteen-year-old boy he thought of as his own son out into the wilderness.

Immediately after Hagar's and Ishmael's departure, Genesis records a visit from King Abimelech, accompanied by the commander of his army. Abimelech said to Abraham, "God is with you in all that you do; now therefore swear to me here by God that you will not deal falsely with me or with my offspring or with my posterity, but as I have dealt loyally with you, you will deal with me and with the land where you have resided as an alien." And Abraham said, "I swear it."

There are any number of reasonable explanations why Abimelech would want to make sure that he was on good terms with a man as wealthy and powerful as Abraham, including simply the rumor of the miraculous child and any lingering suspicions Abraham might have had, but I can't help wondering whether anything about his visit struck Abraham as odd. . . .

The command to sacrifice Isaac is for me the most difficult passage in the entire Bible. I had intended to deal with it by drawing a parallel between Isaac and Jesus, and to note the fact that, in the end, Abraham didn't have to go through with the sacrifice of his "only begotten son," while you did. But now I have to question whether you gave the command at all. I wonder if Abraham didn't rather notice a certain similarity in facial features between Abimelech and Isaac and come face to face with the truth mere moments after swearing never to attack Abimelech without provocation. Suddenly, he was very provoked, but with no desire to declare his justification for war. If not for Abimelech's shrewd covenant, he could have vented his rage without revealing his shame.

It may be that Abraham supressed his rage until he had a horrible idea and said, through clenched teeth, "Hey, Isaac, let's you and me go to the land of Moriah and worship on one of the mountains there. What do you say?"

When they got to the mountain, Abraham told his servants to sit tight while he and Isaac went on. He took only a knife and a torch, and had Isaac carry some wood. Who knows how old the boy was? Old enough to talk and carry wood, possibly much older. He said to Abraham, "Father!" And Abraham said, a shade too loudly, "Here I am, my son." And Isaac said, "The fire and the wood are here, but where is the lamb for a burnt offering?"

And Abraham said, "God himself will provide the lamb for a burnt offering, my son." I shudder to think what he might have added under his breath.

They reached the top of the mountain, and Abraham built an altar, arranged the wood around the altar, bound Isaac, and placed him on the altar. Can you imagine the terror in Isaac's eyes? I guarantee he was not yet living up to his name by laughing. Were you? Laughing, I mean? Did it strike you as funny to watch this drama unfold?

Abraham's eyes were set like flint as he lifted the knife. Gazing dispassionately down upon Abimelech's son, he relished the futile writhing. Now who was the impotent old man? Yes, he had made a covenant with you and Abimelech, but he had made no pact with Isaac, and neither Abimelech nor even you yourself could stop the slaughter of this chosen child. If he could not strike at either of them, he would strike without mercy at this ... pathetic ... this helpless ... weak ... nose like a hawk (like a vulture) ... eyes the same glowing brown as ... as Sarah's.

The altar before him shattered into a hundred shards, but it was only because of his tears. Had he ever loved Sarah as she deserved? His throat felt as though it had been cut. He lowered the knife and slit Isaac's bonds. He lifted the boy from the altar and wrapped him in his arms and wept great, heaving sobs that might never end. Isaac, too, was crying, and what was Abraham to say? "It's okay, my boy, my son. It was only a test. God was testing us. Testing my love. He wanted. God wanted to know if I loved him more than I loved you, because he could see that I loved you more than anything. And I—just now—did you hear the voice of the angel, speaking just then? Saying, "Abraham, Abraham! Do not lay your hand on the boy or do anything to him; for now I know that you fear God, since you have not withheld your son, your only son, from me."

It was a horrible lie Abraham told about you, one that would haunt people's image of you for countless generations, but you forgave him, because he had forgiven you. He had accepted your gift of a child. Best of all, he had taken responsibility for someone who didn't strictly belong to him but who needed him nonetheless. Thus you, in the twentieth generation of Adam's line, had finally found a man who was made in your image, even as that particular branch of Adam's paternal line died out. Your laughter, if you laughed, was of relief and delight, for here at last was a father who lived up to the name.

But make no mistake, something *was* sacrificed on that altar: Isaac's trust in his father. It is the same with us the day we realize our heavenly father has a knife similarly raised over each one of us. The Abba to whom Jesus prayed is the same who accepts responsibility for his crucifixion.

It's questionable whether Isaac would ever laugh again. But this is the world into which you have thrust us, and your presence and your absence alike are terrifying. But I don't wish to leave the reader with the impression that you were absent from Isaac's story, despite the fact that you neither commanded nor interrupted the sacrifice. You were there, in physical form, the whole time. You simply were unable to intervene, what with your horns being caught in a thicket.

Chapter Four:
The Spring

*In which Tamar lies with Judah
and reveals to him
the glory of vulnerability.*

By accepting Isaac as his son, Abraham proved himself more akin to you than to Satan, and so, after Adam's fall led to a brutal, desolate season of winter, spring came at last—a chance to start anew. Because you incarnate in anyone who identifies with you, Abraham was able to be as you unto Isaac, the new Adam.

Like Adam, Isaac was of questionable parentage and had been threatened with death by the person playing his father.

Like you, Abraham decided that it was not good for the man to be alone. He sent his servant to find a suitable companion for him. The servant returned with Rebekah, Milcah's granddaughter, and she comforted Isaac after his mother's death.

One significant difference between the old and the new Adam was fear. Adam didn't gain the wisdom that starts with the fear of the Lord until after he disobeyed. Isaac was wise beyond his years before he was ever tempted. His naked vulnerability came from a circumcision that could not be undone with fig leaves. Perhaps most significantly, he was baptized into his death at an early age and grew up with the belief that you had demanded his life but accepted a sacrifice in his stead.

So when famine came and you issued your one command: "Do not go down to Egypt; settle in the land that I shall show you," Isaac damn well did as he was told. Now, obedience born of fear is a poor substitute for the trust and responsibility you're looking for, but it will do in a pinch, and you could hardly blame Isaac for the fear.

The land you showed him belonged to King Abimelech, who may have been Isaac's father or his half-brother (the son of the Abimelech that Abraham and Sarah knew). In any event, when Isaac and Rebekah fell into the same pattern as Abraham and Sarah, claiming siblinghood instead of marriage, Abimelech was not so easily fooled. He caught Isaac fondling his "sister," and said, "So she is your wife!" and furthermore rebuked them for tempting the men of his land to sin unknowingly against them. He charged everyone in his land to let the two of them be. Of course, it's possible that there are shenanigans in this story as well. The question is, is this the redemption of the Abrahamic "sister-wife narratives," or more of the same? I don't know, but I suspect that Isaac's fear of you was too strong to brook shenanigans. I can't say the same for Rebekah or her sons.

In due time, Rebekah gave birth (with a considerable amount of curséd pain) to Esau and Jacob, twins who got to be a new Cain and Abel, with the difference being that they had responsible parents who weren't so crippled by shame that they couldn't pay attention to their kids. I'm not saying they were perfect parents, but they accepted responsibility, and in the end it made a difference, because, just as with Cain and Abel, there came a time when the elder wished to kill the junior.

When they were young, Jacob swapped Esau a warm meal for his minutes-older brother's birthright. Then, when their father was old and nearly blind, Rebekah conspired with Jacob to steal the blessing Isaac intended for Esau. The plan worked, and Isaac's blessing included the prophesy that his brother would bow down before him.

When Esau found out what had happened, he pleaded with his father to give him a blessing as well, and the anguish of father and son in that moment is excruciating ("Bless me, me also, father!"), but Isaac had poured out his entire blessing upon Jacob. He was able to give only this much to his favorite son: ". . . you shall serve your brother; but when you break loose, you shall break his yoke from your neck." It was little enough, and when Esau left his father, he was ready to spill some brotherly blood.

Rebekah caught wind of his rage, and made the painful choice to send her favorite son away to her brother Laban rather than risk his murder.

While he was away, Jacob learned what it was like to be manipulated. Had he despised his father Isaac for being fooled by a goat's skin? He had been in love with Rachel for seven years. Surely she was constantly in his thoughts as he worked for her hand, and yet he was fooled in the dark into bedding Leah, an act that no more could be undone than Isaac's blessing. And so he had to work fourteen years for his uncle Laban in exchange for both of Laban's daughters. (Let's hope Abimelech was Isaac's father; otherwise this family is getting dangerously inbred.) He, like his adoptive grandfather, prospered greatly in exile, but when you told him to return home, he was sore afraid, on account of his brother's wrath. Nevertheless (and also like his (true, adoptive) grandfather), he obeyed.

As he approached his homeland, he started dividing his property into extravagant gifts for Esau, in hopes of assuaging his brother's righteous rage, and he sent them on ahead. Just as Esau had held his birthright cheap in comparison with his extreme hunger, Jacob counted his flocks and his belongings as nothing in comparison with his life.

Then he sent his family on ahead and spent the night alone, wrestling with an angel who dislocated his hip and renamed him Israel, meaning "contends with God."

The next morning he arranged his family from least to greatest: the maidservants of his two wives with their children; Leah with her children; and finally Rachel, whom he loved, with her son, Joseph. Then he went ahead of them all, finally to face the fury of his brother, who ran at him, fell upon his neck, and kissed him, and they wept. All of Jacob's family bowed down before Esau, and Jacob convinced his brother to accept all the gifts he had sent ahead of him, and in this way they broke their father's blessing and were free of Cain and Abel's curse.

But even that miraculous reconciliation was not enough to bring about the elusive happy ending you so eagerly anticipated, hoping against hope to prove Satan's accusation wrong. Adam's irresponsibility was redeemed when Abraham accepted responsibility for Isaac, and thus the house of Adam and Eve was finally in order, but in the meantime thousands of years had passed during which those tasks for which Adam and Eve had been set apart were never accomplished, and the world had suffered greatly as a result. There was yet more work for you to do in order to redeem the whole world, and so you continued to search for a male descendant that would be able to accept responsibility for it all. For the next generation of that work, you chose Leah's son Judah, a point that easily can be missed in the Genesis narrative, since the leading role of the last thirteen chapters of Genesis is played by Joseph, eldest son of Rachel (who had died giving birth to his younger brother, Benjamin).

Joseph was his father's favorite, and he knew it, and he was pretty insufferable about it, dreaming of his family all bowing down before him, and parading around in the lavish robe his father had given him. Furthermore, he was a suck-up and a tattle-tale. So when Israel sent him to check up on his brothers, and to bring back word of them, his brothers were less than pleased to see him coming.

In fact, they conspired to kill him, and only Reuben, the eldest (and thus, the one who would bear the bulk of the blame), spoke against outright murder, and suggested they throw him into a pit instead. Later, I think, he intended to come and rescue his brother, and perhaps gain some favor in his father's sight. The brothers saw the sense in Reuben's suggestion and acted accordingly: They stripped Joseph of his robe and tossed him into a dry well.

But before Reuben had a chance to play the hero, Judah was struck with an inspiration. Seeing a passing caravan of Ishmaelites, he said, "What profit is it if we kill our brother and conceal his blood? Come, let us sell him to the Ishmaelites, and not lay our hands on him, for he is our brother, our own flesh." So they pulled their brother out of the pit and sold him into slavery.

When Reuben found the pit empty, he tore his clothes (a common practice, back then, symbolizing how naked and vulnerable and grieved one felt). He returned to his brothers and said, "The boy is gone; and I, where can I turn?"

Without necessarily letting Reuben in on the secret of Joseph's fate, they killed a goat, dipped the technicolor dream coat in its blood, and sent it to their father with the message, "This we have found; see now whether it is your son's robe or not." Israel assumed his favorite son had been devoured by a wild animal, and was inconsolable.

So I have to ask: what do you think of Judah so far?
Well—hang on—it gets better.

Judah married the daughter of a Canaanite and had three sons: Er, Onan, and Shelah. He chose a wife, named Tamar, for Er. Every other time Genesis records a parent participating in the selection of a son's wife, she is a close relative. Whether that was true of Tamar is not reported, but can, perhaps, be inferred. But you were displeased with Er (perhaps because he was of Canaanite descent on his mother's side), and so Er died.

As was customary at the time (some believe the story exists to establish the custom), Judah instructed his second son, Onan, to do his duty and beget a son for Tamar, both for her support and to preserve his brother's lineage.

"But since Onan knew that the offspring would not be his, he spilled his semen on the ground whenever he went in to his brother's wife."

While I don't have any idea how or why Er died, Tamar had a pretty good motive for killing Onan herself, and I believe you were happy to accept responsibility for it.

With two sons down, Judah was reluctant to submit his last remaining son to a woman apparently cursed (or possibly homicidal). He told her that Shelah was too young to marry, so she should go live as a widow in her father's house until Shelah got a little older.

In case you're not aware of the fact, I'll mention that childless widows were not particularly welcome house guests back then. They had no prospects, and were (and still are, in many parts of the world) thus seen as a drain on resources. So, as time went on, Tamar (and doubtless her family, as well) grew impatient with the continuing absence of young Shelah.

When she heard that Judah himself would be passing by to shear some sheep, Tamar dressed up like a hooker and put herself in Judah's way. Sure enough, he approached her and said, "Come, let me come in to you," to which she replied, "What will you give me, that you may come in to me?" He suggested a kid from his flock, payable as soon as he returned from shearing, to which she agreed, providing he provide her with a pledge. He gave her his signet, his cord, and his staff, and . . . came into her.

But, when he sent the kid as promised (the goat kid, not his youngest kid, Shelah), she was nowhere to be found, and, moreover, none of the townspeople could recall any prostitutes in that area, so Judah shrugged and moved on. He preferred to give up his pledges as lost rather than risk ridicule by running around trying to pay back a hooker.

A few months later, word came to him that his daughter-in-law had been playing the whore, and was moreover pregnant as a result. So he said, "Bring her out, and let her be burned." But she sent a message to him, accompanied by his pledges, that said, "It was the owner of these who made me pregnant."

Judah responded in the same offhand manner with which he had suggested burning her to death; he said, "She is more in the right than I, since I did not give her to my son Shelah." Then he took her into his household and acknowledged his paternity of the twins to whom she subsequently gave birth.

That's better, right?

Again there was famine in the land, and only Egypt had any food for sale, thanks to the dream-interpretation skills you had given Joseph. Isaac sent all of his sons to buy some, holding back only Benjamin, who was all that remained to him of Rachel.

In Egypt, they met Joseph, disguised as a high-ranking Egyptian. He asked them about their family, and they told him they were twelve brothers, one of whom was "gone," and the other of whom had stayed behind with their father. Joseph, wanting to see his kid brother (and also wanting his other brothers to suffer), accused them of being spies and told them he would not believe they were honest men without proof. He demanded that one of them be left behind as a pledge while they took the food they had bought and went to fetch their youngest brother. So Simeon stayed behind in Egypt while the remaining brothers returned home.

Israel was distraught when he heard this, but he would sooner give up Simeon for lost than risk losing Benjamin as well. Reuben offered up his own sons as pledge for Benjamin's safety, telling Israel to kill them if any harm came to Israel's favorite remaining son, but Israel was no more interested in punishing death with more death than you are.

A year later, the famine was still severe, so Israel told his sons to return to Egypt for more food. They, in turn, reminded him of Simeon and the demands of the Egyptian official. This time it was Judah who offered to bear the blame in his father's eyes forever in the event of any harm coming to Benjamin, and this time Israel was slightly better comforted, since Judah was offering to accept personal responsibility that wouldn't otherwise belong to him. Also, there was no food. So Israel reluctantly agreed to let Benjamin go.

The brothers returned to Egypt, and Joseph, still unrecognized, contrived to make it look as though Benjamin had stolen a silver cup, so that he would have pretext to keep his brother with him in Egypt. As for the rest of his family, well, he didn't much care what happened to them. As far as he was concerned, they were all culpable for his exile, even his father, who had apparently never cared enough to uncover the truth.

But then his brother Judah did something that, so far as I know, was unprecedented in the history of the world. At the end of a long speech in which he explained to Joseph about the promise he had made to Israel, about Israel's grief over the loss of his favorite son, and how the additional loss of Benjamin would kill the old man, he said, "Now therefore, please let your servant remain as a slave to my lord in place of the boy; and let the boy go back with his brothers."

It was the only thing that could have broken Joseph's heart.

Joseph wept, revealed everything to them, told them the famine would continue for five more years, so they had better go fetch their father, and all his household, and bring them to Egypt to settle in the land of Goshen.

Where (one last lie) they all lived happily ever after.

www.ingramcontent.com/pod-product-compliance
Lightning Source LLC
Chambersburg PA
CBHW021452080526
44588CB00009B/814